Owls

of the

Treasure
Coast

Willie Ortiz

ISBN-13: 978-1983721694
ISBN-10: 1983721697

Burrowing Owls

Burrowing Owls are small (10 inches tall and weigh 6 ounces), sandy colored owls with large bright-yellow eyes. They live in grasslands, deserts, and other open habitats. They hunt mainly insects and rodents. Their numbers have declined sharply because of human alteration of their habitat and the decline of prairie dogs and ground squirrels.

Burrowing Owls live in open treeless areas with low sparse vegetation, usually fields or meadows. The owls can be found in grasslands, deserts, golf courses, pastures, agricultural fields, airport medians, and road embankments, cemeteries, and urban vacant lots. They are often associated with burrowing mammals such as prairie dogs, ground squirrels, and tortoises. Breeding pairs of burrowing owls stay near a dedicated nesting burrow, while wintering owls may move around and roost in tufts of vegetation rather than in burrows.

The nest burrow can be several yards long and is usually around 3 feet deep, but size depends on the animal that originally dug it. Burrows tend to make numerous twists and turns, with a mound of dirt at the entrance and an opening at least 4–6 inches wide. The owls line their burrow with feathers, grass, or other materials. Sometimes burrowing owls dig their own burrows, which can take several days. It takes them less time to prepare the burrow for nesting when they use an existing burrow.

Burrowing Owls eat lizards, birds, small mammals but the bulk of their diet comes from insects. Burrowing Owls are not picky eaters and will eat almost anything they can dig up including grasshoppers, crickets, moths, beetles, mice, voles, shrews, dragonflies, giant water bugs, earwigs, caterpillars, scorpions, earthworms, frogs, toads, snakes, lizards, turtles, salamanders, bats, ground squirrels, small weasels, young rabbits, songbirds, water birds, baby ducks, and even young burrowing owls.

Before laying eggs, Burrowing Owls carpet the entrances to their homes with animal dung, which attracts dung beetles and other insects that the owls then catch and eat. They may also collect bottle caps, metal foil, cigarette butts, paper scraps, and other bits of trash at the entrance, possibly signifying that the burrow is occupied.

Owl photographed in Weston Florida

Eastern Screech Owl

Screech owls are about 6 inches long, have a wingspan of 15 inches, and they weigh about an ounce and a half.

Eastern Screech-Owls eat most kinds of small mammals, reptiles, birds, and insects. This owl is agile enough to occasionally prey on bats and can sometimes even be cannibalistic. When prey is plentiful, Eastern Screech-Owls will store extra food in tree holes for up to four days.

Any habitat with enough tree cover will do for this owl. Tree cavities or nest boxes are essential. Eastern Screech-Owls live and breed successfully in farmland, suburban landscapes, and city parks. On the Great Plains, at the westernmost edge of their range, Eastern Screech-Owls live in the wooden land along streams and rivers. Screech-owls cannot survive if all trees are removed but they will readily recolonize once trees are replanted, especially if nest boxes are also provided.

Eastern Screech-Owls in the suburbs may fledge younger than their rural counterparts, probably because their predators are scarcer in the suburbs.

Eastern Screech-Owls do not build a nest. The female lays her eggs on whatever debris is at the bottom of her nesting cavity, be it wood-chips, twigs, or the cast-off feathers and droppings from a previous year's nest. Settling in, she makes a body-shaped depression where her eggs lie. Eastern Screech-Owls nest in holes and cavities but will never dig a cavity themselves. They depend on tree holes opened or enlarged by woodpeckers, fungus, rot, or squirrels. They often occupy abandoned woodpecker nest holes. Eastern Screech-Owls readily accept nest boxes, including those built for Wood Ducks or Purple Martins, and sometimes nest in wood piles, mailboxes, or crates left on the ground.

Barred Owls

Pleistocene fossils of Barred Owls, at least 11,000 years old, have been dug up in Florida, Tennessee, and Ontario.

Barred Owls live year-round in mixed forests of large trees often near water. They live in large, unfragmented blocks of mature forest, possibly because old woodlands that support a higher diversity of prey and are more likely to have large cavities suitable for nesting. Their preferred habitats range from swamps, stream sides, uplands, and contain hemlock, maple, oak, hickory, beech, aspen, white spruce, quaking aspen, balsam poplar, Douglas-fir, lodgepole pine, or western larch trees.

Barred owls are the adult barred owl is about 25 inches long with a wingspan of 41 inches. They weigh 1 to 2.5 lbs. It has a pale face with dark rings around the eyes, a yellow beak and brown eyes. It is the only true owl of the eastern United States which has brown eyes; all others have yellow eyes. Barred Owls do nothing to change an existing tree cavity or abandoned platform nest. They only add lichen, fresh green conifer sprigs, or feathers to a stick platform nest, and they may flatten or remove the top of an old squirrel nest. Cavities measure 10–13 inches wide and 14–21 inches deep.

Barred Owls usually nest in a natural cavity, 20–40 feet high in a large tree. They may also use stick platform nests built by other animals (including hawks, crows, ravens, and squirrels), as well as human-made nest boxes. Barred Owls may prospect a nest site as early as a year before using it. No one knows whether the male or the female chooses the site.

Barred Owls eat squirrels, chipmunks, mice, voles, rabbits, small birds, amphibians, reptiles, and invertebrates. They hunt by sitting and waiting on an elevated perch, while scanning all around for prey with their sharp eyes and ears. They may perch over water and drop down to catch fish, or even wade in shallow water in pursuit of fish and crayfish. Though they do most of their hunting right after sunset and during the night, sometimes they feed during the day. Barred Owls may temporarily store their prey in a nest, in the crook of a branch, or at the top of a snag. They swallow small prey whole and large prey in pieces, eating the head first and then the body.

Baby Barred owl photographed in Corkscrew Swamp Naples, florida

Baby Barred Owl photographed in Naples Florida.

Barred Owl photographed in Brevard County Florida.

Barn Owl

Barn Owls live in open habitats across most of the lower 48 United States and extend into a few parts of southern Canada. These include grasslands, deserts, marshes, agricultural fields, strips of forest, woodlots, ranchlands, brushy fields, and suburbs and cities. They nest in tree cavities, caves, and in buildings. In the Andes they live in ranges as high as 13,000 feet elevation.

Most barn owls are 15 inches in length with wingspans that can range from 30 to 37 inches. Barn Owls eat mostly small mammals, like rats, mice, voles, lemmings, other rodents, shrews, bats, and rabbits. Most of the prey they eat are active at night. Barn owls occasionally eat birds such as starlings, blackbirds, and meadowlarks. Nesting Barn Owls sometimes store dozens of prey items at the nest site while they are incubating to feed the young once they hatch.

Females make a simple nest of her own regurgitated pellets, shredded with her feet and arranged into a cup. Unlike most birds, owls may use their nest sites for roosting throughout the year. Nest sites are often reused from year to year, often by different owls. Barn Owls put their nests in holes in trees, cliff ledges, crevices, caves, burrows in river banks, and in different kinds of human structures, including barn lofts, church steeples, houses, nest boxes, haystacks, and even drive-in movie screens.

Great Horned Owl

When closed a Great Horned Owl's talons require a force of 28 pounds to open. The owls use this deadly grip to sever the spine of large prey.

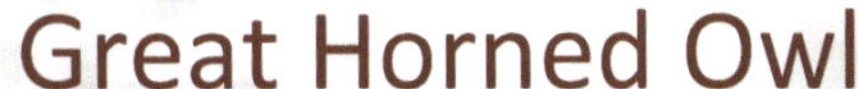

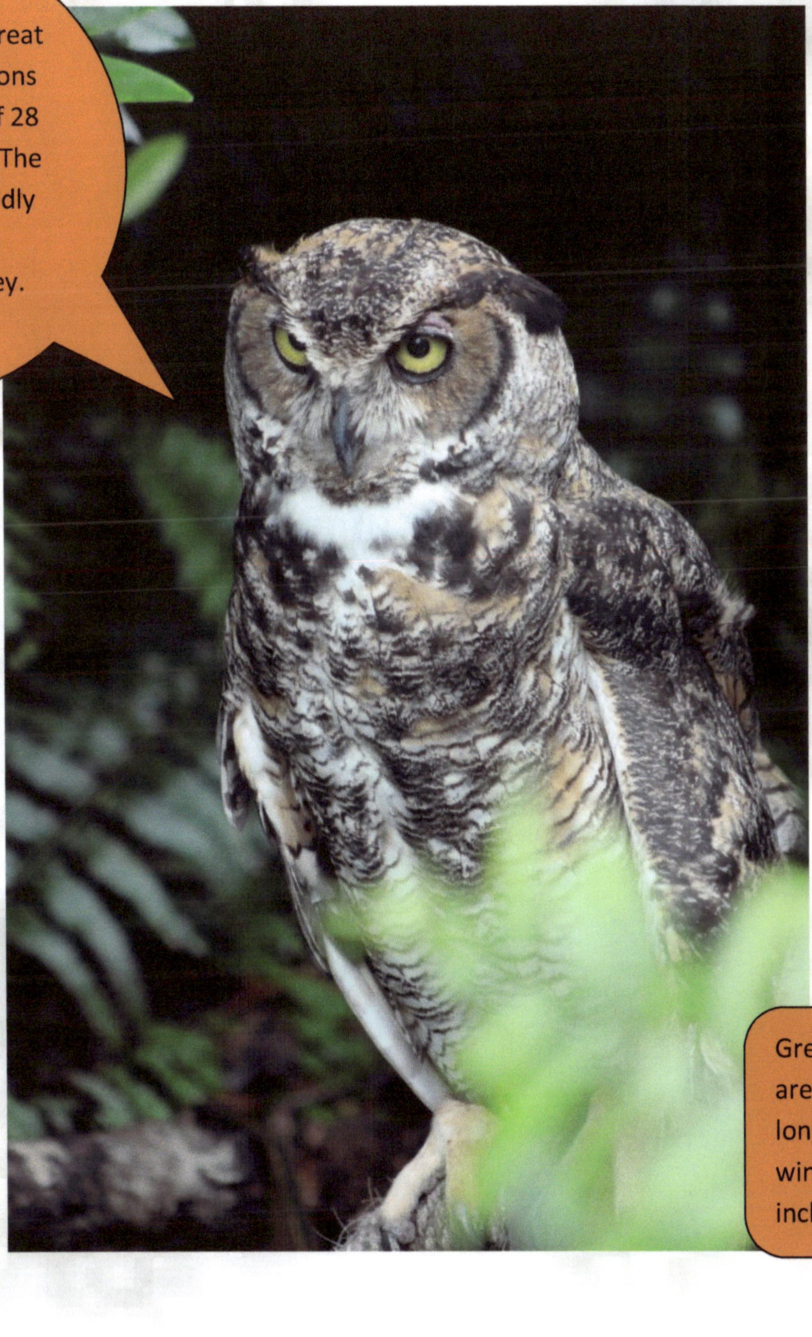

Great Horned Owls are about 25 inches long and have a wingspan of 35-60 inches.

Found across North America up to the northern tree line, Great Horned Owls usually live in secondary-growth woodlands, swamps, orchards, and agricultural areas, but they are found in a wide variety of deciduous, coniferous or mixed forests. In the southern Appalachians, they prefer old-growth stands. Their home range includes some open habitat such as fields, wetlands, pastures, or croplands and forests. In deserts, they may use cliffs or juniper for nesting. Great Horned Owls are also common in wooded parks, suburban area, and cities.

Great Horned Owls typically nest in trees such as cottonwood, juniper, beech, pine, and others. They also use cavities in live trees, dead snags, deserted buildings, cliff ledges, and human-made platforms. In the Yukon they nest in white spruces with witch's brooms (which are clumps of dense foliage caused by a fungus). They occasionally nest on the ground. Pairs may roost together near the future nest site for several months before laying eggs.

Nests often consist of sticks and vary widely in size, depending on which species originally built the nest (hawks, crows, ravens, herons, or squirrels). Great Horned Owls may line the nest with shreds of bark, leaves, downy feathers plucked from their own breast, fur or feathers from prey, or trampled pellets. In some areas they add no lining at all. Nests deteriorate over the course of the breeding season and are rarely reused in later years.

Great Horned Owls have the most diverse diet of all North American raptors. Their prey range in size from tiny rodents and scorpions to hares, skunks, geese, and raptors. They eat rabbits, hares, mice, American Coots, voles, moles, shrews, rats, gophers, chipmunks, squirrels, woodchucks, marmots, prairie dogs, bats, skunks, house cats, porcupines, ducks, loons, mergansers, grebes, rails, owls, hawks, crows, ravens, doves, and starlings. They also supplement their diet with reptiles, insects, fish, invertebrates, and sometimes carrion. Although they are mostly nocturnal hunters, Great Horned Owls sometimes hunt in broad daylight. After spotting their prey from a perch, they pursue it on the wing over woodland edges, meadows, wetlands, open water, or other habitats. They may walk along the ground to stalk small prey around bushes or other obstacles.

Above baby great horned owl photographed in Hobe Sound Florida.

Mated owl pairs are monogamous and defend their territories with vigorous hooting, especially in the winter before egg-laying and in the fall when their young leave the area. Great Horned Owls respond to threats with bill-clapping, hisses, screams, and guttural noises, eventually spreading their wings and striking with their feet if the threat escalates. They may kill other members of their own species. Crows, ravens, songbirds, and raptors often harass Great Horned Owls with loud, incessant calls and by dive-bombing, chasing, and even pecking them. Unattended eggs and nestlings may fall prey to foxes, coyotes, raccoons, lynx, raptors, crows, and ravens. Both members of a pair may stay within the territory outside of the breeding season, but they roost separately.

Above owl photographed in Port Saint Lucie Florida.

Great Horned Owls have large eyes, pupils that open widely in the dark, and retinas containing many rod cells for excellent night vision. Their eyes don't move in their sockets, but they can swivel their heads more than 180 degrees to look in any direction. They also have sensitive hearing, thanks in part to facial disc feathers that direct sound waves to their ears.

Above Great Horned Owl photographed in Port Saint Lucie Florida.

Photographed
in Deming,
New Mexico

The End

About the Author

Willie Ortiz is an avid wildlife, nature, and travel photographer. He has traveled extensively across Asia, Europe, and the Americas to view and photograph animals in their natural habitat. When the natural habitat is almost impossible, Willie is a patron of animal rehabilitation and education centers. Animals of Belize, Willie's first book truly shows the passion he has for protecting wildlife through education. Willie's photography reflects his love of nature and expresses a unique perspective of history, nature, and the world around us. Willie's catalog of books includes children's educational, travel, nature, and history themes. Willie Ortiz is originally from the Bronx and currently resides on the Treasure Coast of Florida.